GW00370961

GRAFFITI
(and other poems)

written by savannah brown
illustrated by ed stockham

To Lauryn —

[signature] xo

to kathy zagar, nathan singleton,
and my parents

for keeping me inspired

CONTENTS

BURGUNDY WALLS

i could see you, little person, in your little house
(those burgundy walls might be mine someday)
talking with all the other little people who you
love enough to watch t.v. with on a sunday night
and pour a coffee for on monday morning
and to hear them talk in their sleep
(through shut doors or
only the layer of clothes or
no clothes between you)
talk in their sleep and cry sometimes

your feet were up on the arm of your couch
(i couldn't see your face)
and you had socks on that your grandma
might have gotten for you
the arm of a couch through a
sharp cornered window in a
geometric room, like a honeycomb in a hive
(frequented by the worker bees)

there were other little people in the photographs
on your wall which the chandelier illuminated
it looked expensive
(the chandelier and the frames
and the way the freshly cleaned
glass panes glistened)
and i thought about how that chandelier light
would look bouncing off of
my own burgundy walls someday
licked by steam from the coffee that i bought
and i poured
for my people or person on a monday morning

there would be people in my
photographs who looked like
the people in yours
(the young people smiling
the old people stately
the family's been traveling
everywhere lately
i'll say with a smile though
i do miss them so but i
have been traveling too)

and i can't quite see to the back of the den
but i'm sure you've got bookshelves packed to the brim
run a finger across, wait and say when
second hand classics, again and again
like you read in school
when things only reached as far as the foot of your bed
and you had no need to think about
the chandelier you might someday own
(when the wrinkles from a million seconds
spent laughing start to show)
no need to consider
the smell of freshly painted burgundy walls
or picture frames

i hope you have a nice rest of your life
in that little house
or another little house
(but they're all the same
coated in a fine layer of fingerprints
and sweat and hushed whispers
dinners and arguments and glances)
and i guess it's funny because
if you hadn't had your living room
light on at dawn i wouldn't have
ever known you existed

i'm sorry for
spying on you

AN OPTIMISTIC VIEW OF LOVE

i could use a million words
to describe your lips but
what about when those same lips
the same skin tugged tight over
your rip cage
the same teeth i like to imagine
being dug into my hip bones
are rotting in the ground
or are nothing but ashes
what could be done then
could they toss
me in the same plot
(or vice versa, i guess
you never know
who will be the first to go)
would you share an urn with me
our particles could mingle
for all eternity
(or at least until
the sun burns out)

HAUNTED

i can measure how sad i am
by how afraid i am of the dark
rather, i mean, what's in the dark
counting heart stops and stomach flops
every stair creak when everyone's asleep
except me and my head and my shaky hands
if i look down the basement stairs
and feel a twinge of terror
urge to run from a nightmare
i know that i'm doing okay
but if i feel nothing
or even, sometimes
feel compelled to throw my body
into the void
it's a bad day
sometimes i am the one haunting the house

A POEM JUST FOR ME

this is a poem just for me
(to celebrate the year i will turn twenty)
from me
to you, a person who doesn't really exist
anymore because i have enveloped you
and now wear your skin
and to her, a person
who (i've been told) will someday devour me

skin doesn't die
it grows and moves and moulds
and every day it lays a little differently
heartache and pain pave
very distinct terrains on a chest
in the same way tears erode laugh lines
branching like canyons
or lightning

but apart from being able to reach a bit higher,
not much has changed
gravity falls similarly
on my back and brain
and still, there is sometimes nothing and still,
i can't help it

sometimes there's everything all at once
and i can't help it
and sometimes i go from nothing to everything
over the course of a couple dreams and battered sheets
damp and heavy with memories
and i can't help that either
you will be disappointed to know that
i haven't yet learned how to ride waves
but i have learned how to tie myself to them
and how to hold my breath
(long enough to let them wash over my nose)
i still have a small ribcage
for inelastic lungs
and in times of lulling stability
i still find myself sleepy at noon
because i can only think
in technicolor with my eyes closed

but then i think about seconds
and the sound a year makes
when it crumbles down around you
and the way old flavors will taste
to an even older tongue
and suddenly i want nothing more than
to exist in this dull for eternity

i can say now and it's now
but as soon as the sound evaporates
the mouth that spoke now
isn't mine anymore
and i'm someone who has lived
one more breadth of a hair than before
and sometimes i wonder how many hairs
separate me from you
and if i could quantify the whole thing,
figure the percentage of change from
one blink to the next
from one connection to the next
from one picturesque sky to the next
then maybe
i wouldn't be so scared of her
because right now i'm certain she's either
a myth
or a monster
or both
and though you are not me,
i think you are just as worried about her as i am
but if she is but half of our stubborn she'll be fine
(though if she is just half our critic
our compulsive, our nerve
she might not be)

and god i wonder how her hair feels
and where she sleeps
and what the last thing her lips touched was
i guess i wonder the same things about you
(even though i recall
your first loose tooth
and talking to the family pets about dying
when you first understood what it meant)
because although all the answers are now sewn
into my veins
timeframes like eyelashes
i can't remember the words
so perhaps, in a way,
all of those things are
somewhere underneath my fingernails
or in the soles of my feet
and i'll just have to wait
until her hair becomes mine
and my fingerprints match hers

you know i'm not very patient
but i also don't have very much
of a choice

ORGANS

i have never had my heart broken
(or sliced)
but i have given it to you,
beating
and dripping with blood
i have passed it straight into
your razor sharp nails
and the dry, calloused
skin on your hands
i am sure you have a craving for
human flesh
but please, please, please
be careful with me—
be kind
and gentle
and soft
with my insides
i have given you the power
to turn me inside out, my dear—
please do not use it

REAL ESTATE

i am my own
i have built myself a one-bedroom,
single-bed home in my bones
with a garden and white picket fence
but if you had sense you'd look close to see
the paint curling off the planks so obviously
i've never understood
why i stain it so religiously
when it'll always be a mess
underneath the fake finesse
but i digress

i keep my lawn manicured
snipped short till i bite skin
and if you ask nicely
step through the land mines
you can come in

we'll enter through the attic
it's a topsy turvy cluttered catastrophe
while some spiderweb-coated
corners and crannies cover the space
other parts are pristine
sparkling, new, unused
but if only i knew what to do
with the walls
short sprawling verses
envelop them all

the heart, i'd say, is the living room
and if you don't mind the palpitations
looming threat of infatuation
occasional lack of motivation
it's not a bad spot to spend your time
while away hours, thinking up rhymes

the ceiling drips with blood, ink
and something that when you
run your fingers through it
feels like nostalgia

the kitchen's too big for just me
hallways too wide
too much space for echoes inside
it gets lonely when you only
have conversations with your
own voice
but i guess i have a choice
i could go if i wanted
share the floorboards with someone
in a place less haunted
but i like it here
and i'm happy to stay in this mess on my own
in this home i have built for myself in my bones

HEAD SPACE

it's neither beautiful nor clean
far from landscape painter's dream
and all the roses, lilacs seem to scatter
few and far between

and in the distance you can see
the empty houses, light posts crowded
panic, panic, we're surrounded
ten and twenty, hundred thousand

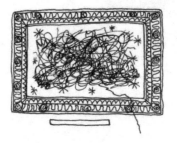

people shouting, woes unfolding
children crying, lovers holding
lovers in their battered hands
asking, pleading, begging, scolding
what will come of all our plans
no one seems to understand

and when it ends, the streets are quiet
city torched amongst the riots
they've all gone to feed the giant
it begins again

I THINK THIS WAS THE FIRST TIME
I FELT LIKE I WAS REALLY LIVING

i told you that
you can feel things better
with your eyes closed
right after i realized that
the back of your throat didn't
taste like booze
and i felt validated
in some strange way that
i'm guessing confused teenagers do

this is a lesson
i told myself after;
a lesson in forgetting
a lesson in disconnect
a lesson in their words are poison laced with sugar
a lesson in you will not have dreams about that smirk
tonight
a lesson in sometimes you can feel it linger after it's gone
a lesson in i like myself better drunk
a lesson in is this what good times are
a lesson in well they were bound to start eventually

maybe i should just
sleep on it

AFTER

i think people are so
infatuated with the afterlife
and so convinced it must exist
because surely it had to be better than this
surely this can't be all there is
like we signed a divine contract
before even entering the womb saying
"your consciousness will be painless
exciting and smooth and light as feather
whether you put in the effort or not
enjoy the ride,"
it said and even in the fine print
nothing could be found
but blind joy and promises of
a future crafted meticulously
with pleasantly warm days and soft safe nights
awaiting you with each rotation of an earth
created for your comfort

like there was a promise it had to be better than this
this can't be all there is, we said
when we were grieving,
depressed and jealous and suicidal we said
this isn't it, this isn't final we said
life's an illusion, death and hate too we said
patience is key and soon we'll be free we said
and every morning you'll dance on
the beach with someone you love
and in sunday school i was told that
if you went to heaven but someone you
loved went to hell you'd forget about them
because in heaven there's no longing
for what cannot be
so i thought
what if they all forgot about me
they'd all still be happy
couldn't even bother to
swallow hard and push it away
but thinking those things is what today's for
i guess
we can be sad now because it'll get better
i guess
but what happens when it doesn't
what a waste

A COLD JOURNEY HOME
ON A SUNDAY MORNING

the ghost of your lips on mine
was the first thing to make
riding the train home
in yesterday's clothes
feel not so lonely
when i saw the pretty people kiss
it didn't sting the same
it wasn't an empty and painful and numb
punch to the stomach
but suddenly the need for oxygen
wasn't quite so urgent
and desperate
as the need to have your hand
wrapped in my hair

I'M COPING

because i inhabit
the same earth
as you
i must subsist
(though you are a
craving to smother
myself in a scent that does
not exist)
i could drown myself in air,
sinking heavy when
your name settles
in the canyons
in my lungs
experiencing a fleeting
moment with eyelids
sewn shut
i could take a photograph
(but those just don't feel
like skin, do they)

THIS CITY IS ALIVE
(DON'T GET TOO CLOSE OR SHE'LL
BREAK YOUR HEART)

this city is alive
this city is alive
and if you don't believe it
inhale and hug her to your
chest
feel the reverberations of her
heartbeat in your stomach
she's a pulsing beating quivering thing
and with every footstep
that echoes through her hollowed alleyways
cobblestoned hideaways
she learns

this city makes no promises
and there's deceit in her mischievous eyes
but the pull of her paradise lips to your own is magnetic
she slams the strongest men
to their knees

she's not a crescendo
she's a bittersweet beauty
a heavy rumbling bass
a numbing buzz
every exhale like rolling thunder

this city is diseased
plagued with chronic loneliness and
the only cure is cigarettes and art

there's a reason spidery veins so closely
resemble aerial night lights
and during the early hours of the morning
the brick almost seems to sigh

MYSTIFYER

i.

    i want you to be my mystifier
    spun from sugar and barbed wire
    sweet to taste but sharp to touch
    oh pretty face, you're too much
    for me today i don't believe
    there's any way you're that naive
    give until i count to three to
    guess the things you do to me

ii.

    i've been having these dreams lately
    that i think are too real;
    in them, i can
    feel the give of my skin and
    the firecrackers in yours
    when you grab me
    and i swear when i woke up i felt
    soft hands around my throat
    i have the careful bruises left
    to prove it

TOO QUIET

i can't even scream to the universe
at the top of my lungs
to ask her what the hell is going on here—
i was told sound can't travel in space
do you think the universe
did that as a joke
and she's right up there ready to listen
but once we get smart enough
to think to enquire
how the existence
of earth has transpired,
we'll learn science said no,
shouts can't reach any higher
than atmosphere level down here.
so we'll fire a rocket! brilliant plan
with an offering and list of questions in hand
"hello!" we exclaim at the top of our lungs
to the universe but she can't hear
so we try again, little louder this time
"excuse me!" we shriek
"i think you'll find this is
as important to you as it is to me"
but the universe can't hear you—
she's sound asleep.

she couldn't have done it on purpose, you see
because with no sound,
she's as lonely as you, even me
who would wish upon themselves such a destiny
when anything in the universe could be done?

so we're alone, i conclude from the lack of reply
it's up to us, i suppose
to find truth the sky

MOLES DON'T THINK ABOUT SPACE OR SMALL TALK

i would like very much to
live in a small hole in the ground
like a mole
a small hole
for an even smaller mole
maybe dug into the side of a hill
and i will close off the entrance
to keep out the chill of the winters,
heat of the summers
no one would know, but please tell my mother
i'm sorry, i'm sorry
but it had to be done
because when you can't run from the
invisible weight of the world
teetering on your shoulder blades
just smother yourself with dirt
bury yourself alive

so at least then you know where the
suffocation is coming from
because when i can feel my stomach
being pulled out through my lips
and forced back down again
whenever it's decided so
i'd at least like to know
who's responsible
so i can thank them for giving me
a gag reflex crafted from steel
and the artistry to construct a
creative, well-rounded list of
a thousand and one ways i could die

i've learned that when fire and ice combine
they don't divide, they multiply
two extremes don't cancel, they intensify
and yes there's something bringing the cold
but oh i bring the burn

if i was a mole
in the side of a hill
i wouldn't seek that same masochistic thrill
that keeps my human heart humming,
human mind numbing
someone please help me,
i think i'm becoming
insignificant again
that's the third time today
a mole wouldn't cry when asked of its day

when i was little i was told
i had an excellent imagination
whoever would have guessed
i'd use it in the creation
of my own personal hell
where everything's my fault
and no matter how small i get
i always take up too much space
while at the same time taking up no space
because have you ever thought about
how big space is
everyone's so small
but i'm the biggest small of them all

not if i was a mole in the side of a hill
with neither the heat nor the chill
it's quiet and cozy
but really, that's silly and i don't suppose we
could come to some sort of agreement
for there's lives to be lived
business to conduct
there's moments to experience
there's nothing to discuss
things to think too much
everything to think too much
i always think too much

ANGRY ABOUT IT

don't ask me what the hell
is happening because
i don't have a clue
//
all i know is
the bitter taste in my mouth
goes away when
your name gets
bounced around in it
acidic lisps, smacking lips
they feel better raw
//
i love you so much
i could cut off your nose
scoop out your eyeballs
and lop off your toes
//
i need to tell
you something
very important
but jesus,
what
were the words

GRAFFITI

maybe if i covered myself with tattoos
or just paint
shot myself with guns filled with ink
and lipstick and perfume
and moved to the city, dressed in graffiti
(both me, and the city)
i could camouflage myself
amongst the grit and the dirt
and i could hide
and then nobody would ever
have to see me again as savannah
but a work of art,
some would call me
is that a banksy, they'd inquire
because they would think
i was made of bricks
or concrete
or bicycle tires
but since i'm made of skin
and not bricks

(although they're both
equally beaten, bruised
and crumbling
marked with initials inside hearts
and scars from what's hit hard
enough to break skin in the past)
no one really
calls those things art
they all say i should try and cover
the marks

RATS

trapped in an abundance of space
they let the street signs swallow them whole
in one pulsating, low-lit, screeching gulp
and they hid under thin blankets
and each other's arms
until they could feel the waves
from the outside's yawn
and with one mighty leap they were at it again;
hand in hand with tired
footsteps on cobblestone and dark smudgy eyes
they emerged into the freezing sunlight to greet the
day with a hopeful gaze
that gave a promise of tomorrow:
that today will pass and
tomorrow, inevitably and gracefully,
will come in the blink of an eye

I DO NOT LIKE THE FEELING

i do not like the feeling of being shaken
i do not like the feeling of my brain
banging against the walls of my skull,
heart flattened in the pit of my stomach
i do not like you
i do not like you
because you are a steel tectonic plate
you are disaster and there is nothing
natural about you
i do not like you
because your laugh is like feather stems
forced through my temples
i do not like the feeling of falling ten stories
my organs escaping
out through my mouth
i do not like the feeling of
weightlessness
i am not in the business of taking bullets,
so i do not like the feeling of desperation
begging to hear gunfire
because you would not forget me then

i do not like the feeling of hollow wrists
fastened to strings
marionette
raising the crushed velvet curtain discovering
silhouettes
whispering like wind chimes
depicting all the times
i could have told you something
i am feeling something
i do not like the feeling of look at me
i do not like the feeling of almost
of almost beds
and almost nights
that you would remember as belonging to me
the nights i won, the nights i was
running from you
just so i could feel
your labored breaths
on the back of my neck

of almost eye locks
i'll shove a key through your socket
i'll crush you
i'll stuff you inside of a locket
i do not like the feeling of irrelevance
i do not like the feeling of smarter than me
of better than me
i do not like the feeling of
no longer queen
i do not like the feeling of dreams
where i'm stood
from a height
and you are the breeze
i swear to god i heard you hiss
i do not like the feeling of being rattled
snake jaw snapped open
i'll swallow you whole

i do not like you
i do not like how your body next
to mine feels like a death sentence
killed by cutting clauses
too accidentally tender
i do not like the feeling of you
in the same way i do not like
the feeling of drunk
swimming in head, scorch throat red
but that doesn't stop me
i do not like the feeling of you
i do not like the feeling
of bones bending to fit your shape
creaking music of decay
you are eating away at my flesh
parasitic picture of perfection
i do not like the feeling
of words trapped in my chest
lungs sticky with smoke and regret
second guess
i do not like the feeling of you

THE ONLY THINGS I KNOW
TO BE TRUE

i know i should clean my room right now
because i mostly think more clearly
without pajamas and mugs
and fifty water bottles spewed across
my bedroom floor
it's likely all those things are dusted in
a solid two-weeks-in-the-making layer
of dust, pencil shavings
and dead skin cells
art may come from tragedy
but i'm not sure it ever came
from mess
this may be the first time
maybe this mess is a tragedy in itself
bless this mess

i know i shouldn't be wishing the days
away but i can't help it
counting down from 24 once
midnight strikes
and then 60
every 60
and i only need to sleep
three more times and
then everything will
finally be okay
i know that's not healthy

but at the same time
if someone told me i was going
to die tomorrow
i wouldn't necessarily regret
spending my last day
lost in my head thinking about
the happy times that await
when you think hard enough
about feeling things
you can almost feel those things
like a warm breeze or an overcast chill
or a kiss

i know i should probably either sleep
or do work
even though this sort of is work
but the nice kind,
not the kind that everyone else says
i should be doing

i know i shouldn't have another coffee
but it looks like that's the direction
the evening is going in
i know this won't help the ever present bags
under my eyes get any smaller
but i've kind of come to terms
with them and i'm happy to let them
live on my face

CLOCK TICK OR A TIME BOMB

everything is beginning to look like you
i spend passing moments carving
your features in the grains on my ceiling
and in trees in the dark
they all have your eyes
so much so
that i can't even recognize
rainy afternoons
or warm blankets in december
anymore because
i'm struggling to remember
when those things had a
distinct identity
and didn't just feel like your chest
falling and rising,
synchronizing like a clock tick or a
time bomb
the nights are the worst
because they remind me how
differently the air shifts when you're near
and how shallow my breaths seem
when you're not

i seldom thought there'd be a time
when it'd be easier to sleep than when
i'm next to you
it turns out, clenching eyes
clutching sheets
dreaming up the smell of sweet sweat
and morning breath
works not nearly as well
but as well as i've got
right now

HEIRLOOMS

my mother taught me that
love is a sense
best enjoyed at arm's length
like a too-loud sound
or a too-hot heat
(heartache hurts because it burns)
though she also taught me that
feeling things too much
is what keeps you alive
(i've got malleable bones
and i could loosen up for you)

my father
taught me that
sometimes the happiness
of others sits lighter on your
eyelashes at night than your own

my father taught me the importance of
a firm handshake
an unwavering confidence to your speech
and possessing the ability to make the strangers
in the room feel as though they've
known you for years

my father taught me that the hands
of anyone who touches me should
be gentle and my mother taught me
that if they are not i should slice
them off
with the blade my father gave me
that i keep underneath my tongue

my mother taught me to not be afraid
to be a shout amongst whispers
and to be unapologetic for the noise
(this is something i am still learning)
my mother taught me that if her presence
feels like a grenade then so
does mine
my parents taught me that some
things do not age
especially
the space behind
your eyes

THREE THINGS I HAVE LEARNED
FOUR THOUSAND MILES FROM HOME

one

you must avoid repetition
whenever you can
doing only things
you've done before
makes it impossible to learn
anything new
you must look the things you are scared of
right in the eyes
and say
i am far too smart
to have something as dull as you
deter me

two

there is more than enough time
to ask a million questions
and then some
try not to worry about
bothering people because
people are kinder
than you tell yourself
and they sometimes know more than you too
(in fact, they usually do)
trust the advice of the experienced
because everywhere you go,
you are a student
you will make more mistakes
than you ever have before
so master the art of vulnerability
and do it quickly

three

you can try and convince yourself
that you are happiest
with a locked door
and quiet to keep you company
but even the most beautiful place
would be a shell without
the echo of laughter
and the sound of a group of clacking
heels on pavement
in the early hours
of the morning
you will sometimes feel safest
with another hand in your own
(independence is not a striving to be alone,
not purposeful seclusion,
but having the strength to say
i'd be o.k. if you weren't here with me
but i'm so glad that you are
and i hope you'll stay awhile)

WORDS OF GODS

the only thing you can
rely on is time
lovers leave
and you tell yourself stories
of could-haves
and should-haves
memories always taste sweeter
years down the line
everyone lies
but everyone dies
and all the streets named
after oak trees that have
been cut down
and the tombstones that have
crumbled away
eroding the names
and the memories
of the living, a bit more faded
and forgotten with each rain storm
all history books rot
even paper containing
the words of gods
disintegrates

nothing is too pure to avoid being
sliced away slowly by each
passing second
there's a comfort in knowing
that there is an end
to each elation and tragedy
there is an end
and i think that is the only thing
we can be sure of

HUM

in the seemingly minuscule moments
before i met you
and in the eternity-seconds after
(even more so)
it was made apparent
(by a part of me i
didn't know had a consciousness—
didn't know could shout so primally
or in those notes
so high and low
i think it's howling)
that i would do everything in my power
to make you hum
you would know every spot
i had been because
they would be marked in
yellow and purple and blue
paint you
silver and gold

thin red rivers stretching down
freckled muscle
i decided, in that heartbeat
that you would never whimper again
in the presence of anyone
(except me)
desperation is not an emotion
i grapple with often
so when i do
i tend to not forget it
you have been
branded
into my scalp
(i could write only
so much poetry
about how i want
you to beg
for me)

NO ANGELS

the way he smells loses its charm
when you realize it's just the smell of
the laundry detergent his mom uses
and the sound of her laugh becomes
a little less magic
when she starts to laugh at you, not with
and in the pit of your stomach
you can feel the plummet,
the rummage, the buckle
of knees against
the weight of the lump
in your throat
when you find out
all that you wrote isn't true
they're just a mistake, mortal like you
their skin can be pierced
(and it normally is)
with regret tied with lace, disinterest post chase
what a day it is when you discover
they're just as not-special
as you think of yourself to be
just as wrong-wired
as you think of yourself to be

no, there's no angels
but yes there is love
it doesn't smell like april
it's not covered with gold dust
encrusted with jewels, smothered in lust
it is there but it's dirty
and under the ground
where the rawest of all of
humanity's found
it's up to you to clean
it up

WORRY DOLLS

i.

you look like my worry dolls
whisper you my troubles dolls
put you in my pillow while your
breaths sing me to sleep dolls

you've got these melodies
that sound like wilting flowers
i'm regretting all the days i spent
counting down the hours

ii.

until i don't even know what
i always figured the weight
of all my fears and nights
i spent crying
would make you shrivel and die

calling me a pesticide
would be too kind
it's herbal homocide
i'm sorry you're unsatisfied
i'm sorry i'm unsatisfied

iii.
i'm not sure who is in
the palm of whose hand
i know you could crush me
with a twitch and a glance
but i think i could
suck out your soul

I'VE WOKEN UP ELSEWHERE

i love that color of the sky
that color of the sky triggered
by puffy eyes and dry mouth
and broken clock
empty docks and harbors
haloed by that kind of pulsing purple sky
that color of the sky in between
a world apart and a world
so recognizable in your bookshelves
and nightstands,
drawers filled with
toothbrushes and chapstick
illuminated by a yellow sky
and leather-bound journals that are only
filled up to the second page
("i know i probably won't write
in this as often as i'd like")

that color of the sky
green radioactive sky
saccharine sapphire sky
red roses pink sky

red and pink don't go
well together most days
but a red pink rose sky
doesn't care about
fashion, really
visions of small town
americana
quiet lulling chatter
ticking beat from somewhere
boiling feet and sticky pillow
open damp windowsill

i feel like i've slept
for my entire life
and have awoken
in the gaze of an
oozing orange sky
where am i
earth doesn't feel
like this